Real Fishing

KEVIN TRUETT

Real Fishing

BAIT & TACKLE MATTER

Real Fishing

Kevin Truett

REAL FISHING

By Kevin Truett
Connection Life Church

210 Liberty ST SE
Salem, Oregon 97301
www.ConnectionLifeChurch.org

This book or parts thereof may not be reproduced in part or in whole, in any form, stored in a retrieval system, or transmitted in any form by an means – electronic, mechanical, photocopy, recording, or otherwise – without prior written permission of the publisher, except as provided by United States of America copyright law.

Scripture quotations marked (NLT) are taken from the Holy Bible, New Living Translation, copyright © 1996, 2004, 2007 by Tyndale House Foundation. Used by permission of Tyndale House Publishers, Inc., Carol Stream, Illinois 60188. All rights reserved.

Scripture quotations marked (NKJV) are taken from the New King James Version®. Copyright © 1982 by Thomas Nelson, Inc. Used by permission. All rights reserved.

Direct scripture quotations from the Bible appear in italic type.

Family photography by Phos Photography
http://www.sierrasphotogallery.webs.com

Copyright © 2015 Kevin Truett
All rights reserved.
ISBN: **1499732112**
ISBN-13: **978-1499732115**

DEDICATION

To the late Dr. J.D. Truett, my father, mentor, pastor, professor, friend, fishing buddy and so much more. My father believed in me and always pushed me to be the very best I could be.

Not only was he a great angler of fish, he was an incredible leader that had no problem being a fisher of men. Growing up, it is very difficult for me to remember any season of my life when there weren't people following my father. He had a gift, and that gift was developing people to be the best they could be.

He was truly a fisher of men and watching him lead the lives of countless people right into the arms of Jesus, well I just had to do the same.

Thanks dad for being my inspiration. I can't wait to see you again. I've got so many more fishing stories to share with you now.

- Kevin

Pastor Kevin resides in Salem, Oregon with Kristie, his wife of 19 years, and their three children, Kameron (18), Keilani (15) and Kennidee (9). Together, with a few family and friends, they launched Connection Life Church and they continue to serve this growing body of believers now located in downtown Salem.

Table of Contents

DEDICATION 6
FROM FRIENDS 11
INTRODUCTION 17
- CHAPTER 1 - FISHERS OF MEN? 23
    A CAN WORKS 27
- CHAPTER 2 - DON'T SCARE THE FISH 33
    DON'T SCARE THE PEOPLE 36
    LADY AT THE WELL GRACEHOUSE 42
- CHAPTER 3 - GET A LITTLE WET 47
    BLACK BOX THEATER 49
    WINE CONNOISSEUR I AM NOT 54
- CHAPTER 4 - GET ALL THE WAY WET 61
    PAPA KAKU 63
    THERE ARE OPEN SEATS AT THE BAR 69
- CHAPTER 5 - ADDITIONAL FISHING TIPS 77
    CLEAN YOUR GEAR 79
    MAKE SURE GOD PREPARED YOUR POND 83
    CHANGE BAIT WHEN THEY'RE NOT BITING ... 85
    LEAVE YOUR GEAR FOR GOD'S GEAR 86
    SET THE TENSION RIGHT 88
    MOVE WITH THE FISH 89

BE PREPARED 90
YOU DON'T ALWAYS CATCH WHAT YOU'RE FISHING FOR 91
KNOW YOUR FISH 92
- CHAPTER 6 - GET YOUR GEAR! 95
FINAL THOUGHTS 101

FROM FRIENDS

"As the World and its turmoil continue to increase, the need for the church to be the light necessary for them to see Christ as the only answer is critical!

Scripture says in (Romans 10:15) 'How shall they preach unless they are sent?' Sending people out into this world to carry the gospel has always been God's way of reaching his creation (II Cor. 2:20) 'Now then we are ambassadors for Christ, as though God did beseech you by us: we pray you in Christ's stead, be ye reconciled to God.'

However, I believe that he puts the responsibility of discipleship on the Church (2Tim. 2:2) 'And the things that thou hast heard of me among many witnesses, the same commit thou to faithful men, who shall be able to teach others also.'

As a Fellow Minister of the Gospel, I can verify that this is a concept that is very much exemplified in the heart and ministry of Pastor Kevin Truett. Over 30 Years I have watched this man of God develop, not only as a Youth Pastor, Senior

Pastor, True Worshipper and Visionary, but I have seen the concept and passion for discipleship personally in Pastor Kevin. His desire to see fellow Christians develop and mature is unprecedented! It is the thrust of his ministry, and those who are familiar with Kevin's heart will tell you this is at the forefront of his life and ministry; reach the lost, disciple the saved and send out the called!

It is with great honor that I suggest and recommend this book, REAL FISHING. I am certain the countless hours spent preparing and writing this book will be of great value by all who read and employ the concepts shared."

Pastor Monte Love
Discovery Christian Center, Portland, Oregon

- - - - -

"I have known Kevin for many years now and I know him to be a very prolific, profound, practical & prophetic communicator & Pastor!"

Pastor Scotty Gurule'
Covenant Generations Church, Tucson AZ

"With the Christian church facing the challenges of an ever-changing world, it is refreshing to know that God is bringing to the forefront "Pastors After His Own Heart", those to whom He has given a new revelation, as well as, a fresh anointing to meet the needs and challenges of His people.

Kevin Truett, Pastor of Connection Life Church in Salem, Oregon, my brother in Christ Jesus and newfound friend, is such a man of God. He has been truly anointed by God to walk in the office of Pastor, Preacher and Spiritual Teacher, taking on the assignment of being on the cutting edge of a hands-on ministry dedicated to advancing the Kingdom of God throughout the world through the preaching of the Gospel of Jesus Christ!

His compassion for the people of God along with his passion for the Word of God empowers his life with a fresh perceptive and insight that speaks healing and hope into relationships and families everywhere, successfully connecting live to Jesus Christ!

Congratulations my friend. May the peace and grace of our Lord and Savior Jesus Christ always be with you as you continue to do the work that God has set before your hands!

Bishop Michael R. Taylor
Presiding Prelate/Chief Apostle
Pentecostal Churches of Truth Fellowship International
Detroit, MI

"I have personally enjoyed my journey and connection with Kevin Truett. Our relationship has developed far beyond Social Media banter and "likes" with regard to ministry tips and ideas!

I have grown to admire Kevin for his entrepreneurial approach to ministry and his desire to "see" vision become reality. Inventive and refreshing, Kevin is impacting his community and this next generation of new leaders!"

Darrell Maston
Lead Pastor, the CENTERchurch, Los Angeles, CA

- - - - -

"I have had the privilege of knowing Pastor Kevin Truett since my junior year in high school. He started Youth on Fire, which was a regional Bible Club outreach to our local high schools. I and several other high school students were very instrumental in helping Kevin with Youth on Fire. He invested a lot of time and energy into developing our leadership skills so that we could succeed at reaching our schools for Christ.

Shortly after high school I became a youth pastor and had the honor of working side- by- side with Kevin in the same city. We did rallies, conferences, camps and leadership training together. Since then I have had the opportunity to partner with Kevin and his church since its inception.

I have shared this brief history of our friendship to let you know that Kevin Truett is the real deal. He is a great friend and an outstanding man of God that lives a life of integrity and excellence. He has a real passion to develop leaders and reach his region with the love of Christ. Kevin is a servant leader. He doesn't just teach leadership principles, he modals them and pours his life into his leaders.

I highly recommend that you take the time to read this book. In this book Pastor Kevin shares insights on how we can position ourselves to receive all that God has made available for us. Your life will never be the same if you will take these principles and apply them."

Marlando D. Jordan

Sr. Pastor, Word of Faith Center, Kennewick, Washington

- - - - -

"Pastor Kevin Truett is a man of God. As my Youth Pastor, he was always ready to help. I never knew of a time when he wasn't ready to serve. He always had a word of encouragement or a thought of excitement for everyone. He was never down and was always ready to help others. He always had a slogan to get you going. It's like his book, POSITION FOR TRANSITION, all you have to do is go for it."

Dr. Roy Roberts
Calvary Ministries, Kennewick, Washington

INTRODUCTION

INTRODUCTION

"Although you can fill a large tackle box with many different types of lures, understanding which lures to use in which situations will make you a more effective fisherman."

Oh how I love fishing. I don't really get out and fish as much as I used to, but I still love getting out there when I can. I have to admit though; I'm not a very patient fisherman. I like to fish in the fishing holes. You know; the holes where all the fish are.

I remember trying to fish in the giant lakes and thinking to myself, "The fish could be anywhere!" But if I found a small fishing hole, I knew the fish had to be right there.

I'm also the guy that has to move if I don't catch something after just a couple casts.

Have you ever been fishing? Chances are you have. I think that everyone I've ever asked has said they've been fishing at least once or twice. Perhaps as a kid you went fishing with grandpa. Or maybe you're an avid fisherman today and you try to get out every weekend. For me, I loved to fish when I was younger and I still love fishing today.

As a kid, I spent many years in the bay area of California. I vividly remember a small community park in Hercules, California and this park had a huge lake right in the middle of it. Wait, maybe it wasn't huge. In fact, now being older and wiser, I might say it wasn't a lake at all. It was more like a pond. Of course, anytime you tell a story about fishing, you seem to remember things to have been much larger than they truly were. Plus, I was very young and being all of 5' tall and 100 pounds plus or minus a couple - - dozen pounds, everything looked huge to me. But my apologies, I've digressed.

I remember fishing in this pond and we loved catching whatever was biting. Most of the time we caught tiny bluegill, sometimes we'd catch a nice crappie or two and if we were lucky, we might have caught a catfish or bass lurking around our big fat juicy earthworms.

My buddy and I used to go exploring back then and we'd find these hidden creeks running through trees and right through town. I won't tell you that we used to take off on my little sister's pink Huffy bicycle because that would just be embarrassing. But when both of our bikes had flat tires, we grabbed our poles and borrowed someone else's bike. Again, I don't want to say whose bike we borrowed or what color it was but we were cruising.

Once we got to the creeks, we would walk carefully and often see giant fish that I can only describe as looking like giant barracudas with enormous teeth protruding out of their mouths. We would drop our lines right in front of these monsters and they would ignore our bait every time. Really, they acted like they never saw our bait. But we always had a blast trying to catch them. These are memories I'll never forget.

In this book, REAL FISHING, you'll read about many fishing stories that may make you laugh, may make you gasp or may just make you think about life a little bit differently. Whatever each story might offer, I do hope you see that, although it is possible to just throw a hook in the water and sometimes catch something, REAL FISHING is a skill and it's a skill that can be learned.

Using the right bait and the right tackle does matter. And if you don't pay attention to a few important details when you fish, you may get lucky here or there, but you'll never catch the fish you're really hoping to catch.

You see, my buddy and I were always fishing for that monster with the mouth full of teeth. But we always hooked the little bluegill or other annoying tiny fish that did nothing but consume our bait and tie up our lines. We spent most of our day reeling these fish in, getting them off our hook and putting new bait on. Very little time if any was spent on the fish we desired to catch.

Of course by now, you may be thinking you bought the wrong book and this book should have been on a shelf at your local sporting goods store or displayed on a dusty end cap in the sporting department of Wal-Mart. It certainly doesn't sound like a book you would buy at church or in a class on leadership.

Well, do not worry. You absolutely have the right book in your hands and no, you did not unknowingly sleep walk to the sporting goods department of Wal-Mart in the middle of the night on a mission to become the best fisherman in the world.

REAL FISHING is going to offer real fishing stories that can be applied to our everyday lives as we seek to make disciples, influence others and connect with them in genuine ways.

I'm going to share with you a few real fishing strategies that can be applied to how we reach people. How we really can be fishers of men and make true disciples. These tips can also be coupled with your recruiting strategies when trying to hire that ideal employee or when trying to find that person that will eventually take your place.

So sit back and enjoy the stories. And let me say, the stories you are about to read are not all mine but they are all 100% true to the best of my knowledge. They may be fish stories, but I've made every effort to keep it real. And if you apply the REAL FISHING strategies outlined in this book, you'll have stories of your own and will look back one day simply amazed at the accomplished angler you have become, in water and on land.

Let's go fishing.

- CHAPTER 1 -
FISHERS OF MEN?

Fishers of Men?

A few years ago, God gave me a sermon series called, "Going Fishing." When God was speaking to me about that series, He started showing me some things that we may have all known our entire lives, but as I was preparing my notes for this series, it all began making sense to me like never before.

In Matthew 4:19, Jesus said He would teach normal fishermen to become fishers of men. Fishers of men? What could that possibly mean? You can't hook a man's lip with a hook. Well, I guess you can and some men have, but it hurts an awful lot. And if you hook them without their consent, I'm pretty sure there will be trouble. I'm pretty confident; no man is going to give you their consent. So, let's assume a total accident. Even if you did hook a man, you can't eat them. That's extremely gross not to mention highly illegal. Surely the rules of fishing for men would have to reflect some sort of catch and release requirement.

Fishers of men? What could He have possibly meant by saying such a thing? I mean, these guys had legitimate careers in the fishing industry. Were they being mocked? Were they being tricked?

Not hardly.

Jesus was on a mission and He wanted to recruit some help. Here He finds a few guys that know a little something about fishing. So He uses their skills, their livelihood, and their comforts to draw them in.

In a sense, Jesus was fishing for men and then teaching them to fish for men as well. And the bait He used? He simply used terminology these guys could relate to.

He was already known for drawing crowds and leading masses of people at will. He appeared to be the best of the best. He was successful at what He did and every fisherman wants to know your secrets.

Could you imagine if someone like Michael Jordan happened to be walking near the park where you and the guys (or gals) were playing some ball in a quick pick up game? Now, try to imagine him walking up just as you go in for the perfect layup. He stops and watches, then looks at you and says, "Leave this park, follow me and I will make you a professional basketball player in the NBA."

Michael Jordan, in the opinion of many, was and still is the greatest NBA basketball player in the history of the sport. If you wanted to be a basketball player and he offered to make you successful playing basketball, most people would drop everything and go.

Imagine if Arnold Palmer said, "Drop your clubs, follow me and I will make you a professional golfer in the PGA. If you enjoy the game of golf and desire to be successful, most would quickly drop their clubs and follow.

These men that Jesus was talking to, they were fishermen. They spent their lives learning how to lure fish, how to draw them in, how to hook them and how to get them in their boat. What Jesus was offering wasn't much different. I'm sure the way He communicated this offer to the guys probably sounded quite appealing.

At a very young age, I knew I would be one of those fishers of men. It took me a while to get serious about it, but I knew it would happen one day. My daddy was a fisherman, my grandpa was a fisherman and my great grandpa was a fisherman. I came from a long line of fishermen. All of them started as fishers of fish and eventually followed the call to be fishers of men.

My father was one of the greatest fishermen that I've ever known. It was extremely rare that he came home after fishing and didn't bring any fish home with him. He even fished without always having the proper gear. But he didn't let a lack of gear ever stop him from fishing.

A CAN WORKS

One day, dad took us all to Lucky Peak Dam to go fishing, just outside Boise, Idaho. I remember heading up to the lake and I didn't see that we had enough fishing poles, but we were going anyway. I just assumed we must be sharing. When we finally got to the sandy shore that we wanted to fish, we made the hike down and setup our area. I was right; we didn't have enough fishing poles. I don't think mom ever really liked actually fishing, she usually came along just to hang out, and so we didn't have to worry about her. I certainly made sure I had a pole and my sisters were pretty young so it wasn't difficult to beat them to the gear. But I noticed my dad didn't bother to string up a pole for himself.

Instead, I saw my dad begin to tie some fishing line to the tab on his Dr. Pepper can. I was curious to what he was doing, but that day dad taught us that we could fish with a can, a line and a hook.

So I continued to watch my father as he prepared his gear that basically came out of our cooler. He tied his line to the tab of his can and started winding the line gently around the can. He made sure not to smash the can in the process and he had plenty of line to wrap. Once the line was on, he left some excess and tied the end of it to his hook. At this point, the line setup was exactly the same as always.

He used a hook, a weight and a bobber, just like my setup. The only difference, he was using a can while I used a fishing pole.

I thought; there was no way that was going to work. You need to feel the fish and you can't feel the fish without the right pole. But my father insisted he would out-fish me.

So it was "Game-On!"

I finished getting my line ready and I cast it out just perfectly.

My dad held the excess line in his right hand and the can in his left. He began swinging his line around and around like a sling shot. And with just the right momentum, he let go and launched his line into the lake landing it right next to mine.

I could only think, "Impressive!"

I proceeded to set up my pole on a "Y" shaped stick to prop it up. Then, I waited.

My father started pushing sand with his hands and appeared to be building a sandcastle on the shore. I watched intently with great curiosity. And then I saw that he wasn't building a sandcastle at all. He was building a mound of sand to hold his can.

I still didn't understand how he was going to catch a fish when you have no pole to watch bend. But then it happened.

As we were both sitting on the shore anticipating the first catch of the day, I saw my dad's can jump right off the mound of sand he built and then it took off bouncing along the shore line and heading toward the water.

My dad jumped up and ran for the can. For his age, I thought he could get around pretty quick. He eventually caught the can and yanked it above his head. I just began laughing while I watched my dad start winding his line around his can again. And when the line was all nicely wound around his can again, I was amazed as I laid my eyes upon a real live fish on the end of my dad's line that he was proudly holding up to show us all.

He then looked at me and said, "A can works."

"I suppose it does." I replied.

That day, my dad didn't just teach me to fish with a can. He taught me how to improvise. He taught me how to be successful without always having the latest and greatest equipment.

He had the right bait and he used the right tackle. The pole didn't really matter. It wasn't the pole that was important; it was the bait and tackle.

My dad was a preacher. He was a fisher of men. And we didn't have the latest equipment, we didn't have the most expensive buildings, but what we had was the right bait and the right tackle.

When I refer to bait as it relates to being a fisher of men, I'm simply referring to the "stuff" that draws them in. I'm not at all suggesting that we use "bait" meant to lure or trick them into biting.

My dad taught me that day at Lucky Peak what it really meant to go fishing even without all the fancy stuff. And that's how he was building the church. That's how he was recruiting disciples and that's how he was growing his team.

A can works.

That fish he caught at the lake that day was a large steelhead; the largest fish of the day.

In dad's business, he always had followers. I remember a long run in Amway. Dad and mom always had a growing down line.

In his church, he always had followers that loved him and that were quite loyal. We didn't have the largest church in town, but we had a growing group of disciples that wanted to grow the kingdom together.

Dad didn't always have the latest and greatest, but he learned to fish with what he had and he learned to catch people with his vision and with the gifts that God blessed him with.

Whether in business or in ministry, God has gifted you with talents and skills. He wants you to be successful and He always includes provision to fulfill vision.

NOTES

- CHAPTER 2 -
DON'T SCARE THE FISH

Don't Scare the Fish

There are many ways to fish, but I want to highlight just a few. One of the most difficult ways to fish for many is to send your gear out to where the fish are but keep your distance so you don't scare the fish away.

If you're a hunter you'll understand this concept well.

You can't just run into the woods waving your gun around, breaking branches and making all kinds of noise. You would certainly scare all the game away and go home empty. I know from experience. With many years of hunting with my dad I remember him yelling at me with his whisper to "Stay quiet! Watch where you're stepping! Shhh!" Have you ever been yelled at with a whisper? Dad didn't want me scaring away the deer.

Unfortunately, I remember coming home empty more often than not and fishing can be the same way.

When you want to catch the big fish, the right fish, the fish you want in your net, you need to sneak up on them. Otherwise you are likely to scare the fish and not catch a thing.

I enjoy this type of fishing. I like to hike quietly up the river banks watching for activity in the water. I like to keep my distance and cast up to where the activity is.

I recall a fun hunting trip with my brother-in-law and our boys. We went to Imnaha where the game was thick and the fishing was great. We took a break from hunting one morning and I took the boys fishing.

We hiked and hiked right up the river. We were on a mission to bring dinner home in the form of trout and I was the leader of this mission. We went up the river in formation and we were stalking our pray.

Every so often, we would see some activity in the water ahead of us and we would stoop down. We used our whisper voices and we strategically cast ahead keeping our head and our bodies out of the line of sight.

By doing so, the fish didn't even know we were coming. We cast our lines right to them and before our rigs could even hit the water, these fish were jumping at the chance to chomp on our flies.

We ended up catching so many fish, we had to start letting them go and keeping only the biggest fish that would make the best meal back at camp.

DON'T SCARE THE PEOPLE

Several years ago, I felt like God wanted my church to begin praying for our community leaders. We've always prayed for them, but now we were to step it up.

We decided to target high profile business leaders in our communities as well as city and state officials. We would choose one each week and we would publicly pray for them during our Sunday worship service.

We also started printing several prayer points in our bulletin or weekly church program including this important point to pray over these leaders. After praying for them in our worship service, we then send a personal letter of appreciation to these leaders and we send them a copy of our weekly bulletin to let them know that our entire church is praying for them this week.

We are still doing this today and as a result we have had the privilege of praying for all of our government officials and countless non-profit organizations and local businesses that are making a difference in our communities.

I love seeing the letters land on my desk or my inbox when these leaders, many whom we have never met in person, write me to personally say thank you for the prayer.

One Chief-of-Police was moved enough to admit to me the difficult challenges of his job and how he desperately needs a prayer covering. He went on to say that our point of prayer and the letter he received from us could not have come at a better time. Knowing that we were praying for him that week was enough to give him the encouragement and strength to continue on.

Another letter of appreciation I received was followed up by a phone call to my office from the president of a local charity we prayed for. He was so touched by the fact that our church was praying for him and expressing appreciation that he wanted to meet me in person.

We met for coffee and as a result partnered together in future events to feed hundreds of families if not thousands that were less fortunate and hungry.

I can tell you story after story how this strategy has worked for our church. We were throwing our line out to these city leaders but we were throwing them from a distance. We never knocked on their door or called them. We aren't making noise or publicizing our actions. We simply prayed for them and let them know we were praying for them. We expressed our appreciation for the role they play in our community and we let them know that we are available and will continue to pray for them going forward.

We had (and to this day still have) absolutely no expectations on those we pray for. Our intention is to bless our community without any strings attached.

Now let's think about what might happen if I gathered 100 church members and marched up to our capital building making a lot of noise praying.

What do you think would happen at the office of the Police Chief if a huge group of us marched up and asked to see him?

Chances are we would be escorted off the property and asked to not come back. We would not make a very good impression on the leader we're praying for and our effectiveness would be very limited if not nullified completely.

Instead, we're keeping our distance. We don't ask for anything in return and they don't even see us coming. Then out of nowhere, they receive a letter of appreciation and prayer.

Some companies sneak into a market. They don't make a bunch of noise. They just drop hints. They come in a little stealthy.

I remember my family wishing for a Sonic Drive-In restaurant in Salem for years. They absolutely love the Cherry Limeade drink. Then one day, we started seeing a few commercials for Sonic on television. This really upset my wife and kids because they love Sonic but we didn't have one. Why would they play commercials on our local stations? We asked a few locals about what they thought of the commercials and to our surprise they often asked, "What's Sonic?"

Almost a year later, Sonic moved into Salem with two locations and are quite successful. The quiet move to play a few commercials here and there nearly a year before they even arrived, was a strategic way of peaking the public's curiosity.

Basically, they were throwing lines from a distance directly into our community. And the fish, I'm sorry, people were going nuts.

Less than a year ago, I started seeing billboards on the streets of Salem with a big Q looking logo on them. That's it. No message, no name, no location. Just a giant logo that looked something like the letter Q. Not long after noticing the billboards, I noticed the same logo on window decals appearing on cars. Still no name, just the logo but now a message saying, "It's coming."

I had never seen this logo before then and my curiosity was peaked. This went on for nearly six months and then it arrived. A large exercise gym on the South side of town opened up. The name? Physique. The logo? A big Q. At least I think it's a Q. At this point, it really doesn't matter. My sister and her entire family are members and they work out there daily. My sister talked with my wife and she is now a member. My mother is a member and many of our church members are now working out there getting their bodies in shape. It appears like this exercise company had experienced instant success. This is really impressive since there are many other exercise gyms in our community that existed long before this one. There is certainly no lack for competition.

So how did they reel in so many new members?

They came at us from a distance. They peaked our curiosity. They didn't make a bunch of noise; they quietly dropped a few lures in front of us before we even knew they were coming. I'm quite confident that if they just moved right into town, bought a few billboards and opened their doors, they wouldn't be half as successful as they are.

Sometimes you have to fish from a distance. Don't scare the fish. Just drop the lure in front of them. Learn to cast from a distance.

The last time my son and I went fishing, we practiced in our front yard. We had no water in our front yard, we just practiced casting. We would aim and cast, aim and cast. We wanted to be able to cast from a distance. Of course, we needed a little more practice. I don't remember if it was my son or I who cast into our neighbor's tree... across the street! One of us got hung up! We were snagged! We walked across the street and then discovered we were snagged up high in their tree. There was no way we could reach it and it wasn't a tree would could just climb up. We had to cut our line and it was pretty obvious that our "casting from a distance" skill was a little rusty.

To this day, I'm not sure our neighbor knows why there is a lure up in his tree.

LADY AT THE WELL GRACEHOUSE

Laura Allran has been attending our church for over a year now. She is the Executive Director and Founder of Lady at the Well Grace House, a temporary shelter for women in transition.

Just before she began attending our church, she and her organization became the target of our prayer points. We prayed for her from a distance and simply sent her a letter of appreciation for the important work she does in our community.

Here is how it impacted her.

Laura Allran

This first time I heard about Connection Life Church was when we received a letter from them stating that they will be praying for us in their church service. It was during a time when we were just getting Women at the Well Grace House started so we needed many prayers. As our Executive Director read the letter at our board meeting, I felt like I wanted to visit the church to check out the church that was actively and effectively being the hands and feet of Jesus. When I arrived at Connection Life Church, I was welcomed with open arms and greeted with so much love. The worship was a beautiful connection with God and the Word was edifying. During the service, a few of the members came up and prayed for a Salem leader, Salem organization, and another Salem church. I was impressed with their efforts to extend their prayers to others outside the church and support their community. I believe that it was because of their prayers and continuous prayers that Grace House opened and is still running today changing the lives of homeless women in the Salem community. Since then I considered Connection Life my home church and I have gained so much from being there. Although I have moved away, the Pastor and other members of the church still reach out to me with love. I am gratefully thankful for this church and affect they are making to the Salem community.

- Laura Allran

We never invited Laura to attend our church. We didn't pray for her with an expectation that she would recognize our church and begin attending. We prayed for her to make an impact from a distance.

Sometimes the fishing we do from a distance has a greater impact than trying to get up close and personal.

The reality is, we weren't fishing for Laura. But as a result of our strategy to serve our community from a distance, Laura became a welcomed part of the Connection Life Church family.

NOTES

NOTES

- CHAPTER 3 -
GET A LITTLE WET

Get a Little Wet

Sometimes fishing from a distance is not always possible. There may be several reasons for this. Perhaps there's too much in the way and not enough room to cast properly. Maybe there's not a clear path to quietly approach the fish you're trying to catch.

Whatever reasons might prevent you from using our first fishing technique; there are still a couple more ways to be successful.

Another way to bring home a full stringer requires you to get a little wet. You may have to walk out into the water just a little bit. The water is often cold and at first quite uncomfortable. It usually takes a couple minutes to get used to it.

I actually don't mind this kind of fishing. The closer I can get to the fish, the better. Even in the coldest weather, we just put our waders on and got out there where the fish are. Sometimes the fish would swim right by us and occasionally they would even brush our legs. Those were incredibly exhilarating moments.

BLACK BOX THEATER

In October of 2012, our church moved into a theater in downtown Salem, OR. This theater was what people often referred to as a Black Box theater. I believe it had to do with the fact that the entire stage was painted black and the stage wall was also painted black.

For a church this seemed a little unusual, but with the right décor and proper lighting, this theater became our home.

One of the advantages of occupying this theater was the fact that we could maximize its functionality by opening it up to our community for theater productions, concerts and recitals, etc… That year we decided to launch 2nd Floor Productions. We scheduled all kinds of entertainment to come in once a month and typically had no problem filling all the seats with an audience.

What does this have to do with fishing?

Well, the majority of our events were secular events, produced and presented by me and my church staff. We had one rule and pretty much only one rule. The rule was that no artist could blatantly oppose our Biblical principles and teachings. We knew that many of the artists weren't Christians and many probably didn't believe what we believed, but as long as they didn't come in with their own message that directly opposed our beliefs, they were welcome to perform on our stage.

Every artist we invited was very understanding and respectfully agreed. Likewise, we agreed to not push our church or our own agenda on any of their audiences. Our goal was simple; serve our community without expectation of anything in return and make genuine connections in our community through the arts and entertainment.

The results were amazing. My staff and I put our waders on and we got in the water a little bit. Many Christians would strongly oppose participation in such secular events. Long ago, it was considered a sin in most church circles to even go to the movie theater. But we knew we had to get into their environment just a little bit. And that's exactly what we did.

In the middle of downtown, our church decided to maximize the opportunity of occupying a true black box theater. We decided to obey God and trust God. The musicians that performed, the entertainers that graced our stage, the community that enjoyed it all; everyone was coming together, those that believed in God and those that didn't. The one thing we all had in common was a mutual respect and love for the arts.

This was enough to cause many people among the entertainers as well as the entertained to approach me after each performance and ask for more information about our church and some specifically asked about God and who He really is.

I remember one evening of classic rock and roll that led to a nearly thirty minute conversation about God and ministry with one of the band members that had just performed.

This gentleman remembered church as a kid, but never really spent any time in church after moving away from home. He did believe in God and the fact that I was a pastor and took the time to connect his band with the community without pushing religion down anyone's throats; well it gave him hope again. After his performance, we sat together in the front row of this black box theater, which also just happened to be the front row of my church, and talked about God and forgiveness.

Another secular pop rock concert we hosted was preceded by a lengthy conversation between the lead singer and me. I noticed during setup he was staring at all of the posters on my office walls. These posters were sermon series title posters that were colorful and eye catching. It didn't really surprise me that he would be checking them out, but what happened next really blew my mind.

Just before it was time for me to take the stage and introduce the band, he tapped me on the shoulder and asked if he could speak to me in private for a moment.

I thought it was odd that he would ask to chat with me just minutes before show time, but he was the lead singer and I assumed whatever he was about to request must be pretty important.

We walked out of the theater toward my office and he stopped us right in the middle of the hall. He then began to share with me with tears beginning to fill his eyes how he knew without a doubt that he was supposed to follow God and use his talent to minister to people.

At this point, tears began to fill my eyes and I forgot all about our black box theater packed with fans waiting for the lead singer to come on stage. I placed my hand on his shoulder and began to assure him that God had a plan for his life and his music.

He shared with me the story of his life and how he and his family had been so hurt by the church in the past. He grew up in church and only remembers the hypocrisy, the back stabbing and the pain the church caused him on many occasions. He grew to resent the church and decided to pursue his career as a musician.

Now we're at least 10 minutes past show time and I'm pretty sure my staff was wondering what in the world was going on. The band was patiently waiting wondering where their lead singer was and the fans were probably wondering if the lead singer got sick and they were about to get a refund.

But, after just a few more minutes of speaking into this man's life, I asked him if I could pray for him right then. He didn't even hesitate to let me lead this prayer and we prayed together right in the hall way with a packed theater just on the other side of the door.

After praying together, he gave me a very strong hug accompanied by very vocal thanks. Then we both re-entered the theater and I took the stage to introduce him. Of course I apologized for the delay and said, "Let the show begin!"

Everyone erupted with cheering and we had one of the best shows of the year that night.

This experience doesn't happen unless we're willing to get a little wet with the fish we're trying to catch. My staff and I had to put our waders on and get in the water a little bit with these artists. Once they saw that we had no interest in judging them for where they were in life and that we didn't mind getting a little wet with them, they let down their guards, forgot we were in my church and genuine connection were allowed to be formed.

WINE CONNOISSEUR I AM NOT

In the last days of my father's life, I took a temporary job at one of the largest financial institutes in the world. I was just a temporary admin guy on the lowest part of the totem pole. My job was very simple; field messages for top executives in the bank and forward the important messages to the correct executives if it met a certain criteria.

I arrived to work around 9:00PM and ended my shift at 6:00AM. I cannot recall why we had to work this overnight shift, but that's what we did, me and about 11 other temps assigned to this job.

This was a two week gig for me that only paid about $12 per hour. But, this job was necessary for me to be able to stay with my dad while he was in the hospital. With the flexibility of this job, I had to take it.

Well, dad passed away and this two week gig got extended two more weeks, then two more months. And every time they extended my contract, they gave me a raise. I certainly didn't mind.

Fast forward five years and I was still a contractor, but now a project manager for this giant financial institution now earning over $150,000 per year. Not sure how that happened with no education in this field and no training in project management. But here I was in the midst of all the big guys.

I found myself often working side by side with the Vice President of the corporation and shaking hands with the very men and women that keep this corporation breathing.

Well, during my season with them, I was called to travel quite extensively. The projects I was responsible for had budgets in the tens of millions and more. And at times, I found myself staying in the nicest hotels with the nicest limousines taking my team from restaurant to restaurant.

Why am I telling you all this?

While God was blessing me financially and I found huge favor in this job, my wife and I were also the pastors of our first church. And I didn't hide this fact from any of my colleagues. In fact, I was often called upon to pray over the meals and give Godly counsel to others on the team that were going through "stuff."

Through all of this, my bosses often took us to fancy restaurants and high end wine cellars. It seemed like everyone I worked with had a knowledge of wines as if they went to school for it.

And then there was me. Growing up, I never touched alcohol or tobacco. Wait… I take that back. I did experiment with my aunt's already smoked cigarette one day that she left in her bathroom. I tried to light it to see what it would be like to smoke. I filled my cheeks with my first puff and never touched another cigarette again. I thought I was going to die and I was sure that if I did I was going straight to hell. Ha! Never again.

So here I was in the midst of a bunch of wine connoisseurs that was smelling, swirling, swishing and assessing every glass. They decided they would educate me and I felt like I was way out of my comfort zone. But, I was a pastor who wasn't afraid to get a little wet.

Please don't get me wrong, I'm not talking about indulging in a sinful nature. I'm not talking about going back to that childhood day when I sneaked a puff of my aunt's old cigarette in her bathroom. I just wasn't afraid of being exposed to the cold elements of the world when I knew I had God on my side keeping me safe and warm.

So my non-judgmental approach and my ability to "get a little wet" in order to win the trust of my colleagues allowed me to minister to them in ways no one else could.

They weren't calling any local pastors or chaplains to help them with their lives, but they had no problem calling me. Little did they know, I was fishing every day while earning a great living meeting the needs of this TOP 100 Company.

If you won't get a little wet sometimes, you just might miss out on some amazing opportunities to catch fish you've never even seen.

> [1Corinthians 9:22-23 NLT] 22 When I am with those who are weak, I share their weakness, for I want to bring the weak to Christ. Yes, I try to find common ground with everyone, doing everything I can to save some. 23 I do everything

> *to spread the Good News and share in its blessings.*

I can't emphasize enough that this passage isn't a free pass to indulge in a sinful nature. This type of fishing requires a tremendous amount of discipline and strength.

During this fishing trip, I was amongst high profile executives and I did everything I could to earn their trust and their respect. I put my waders on and got in the water where they were swimming.

After five years of wading where the fish were, I didn't have to go after them, they were coming to me. Just like I often saw in the Boise River; fish would get so comfortable with me in their environment that they would literally come to me and brush right up against my legs.

I didn't judge my colleagues and I didn't make a big deal about their evening environment. I wasn't a party pooper and I let them share their interests with me. Of course I didn't go in unprotected. I was prayed up and I had my waders on. I truly believe this is what opened up the door for authentic relationships and authentic ministry.

NOTES

NOTES

- CHAPTER 4 -
GET ALL THE WAY WET

Get All the Way Wet

Then there are the times when you just have to go all the way in. You need to put a full suit on and get completely in the water. Not a three piece suit; a wet suit. You need to put on a suit that will keep you from dying of hypothermia; a suit that will protect you from the elements you are about to subject yourself to.

In Boise, Idaho I used to love fishing in the winter. It wasn't always easy as temperatures would often drop below zero and I vividly remember the winter of 1986 when my father and I rolled into town with our green station wagon pulling a beat up U-Haul trailer and it was 40 below zero. Regardless, when we wanted to fish, we bundled up, stepped out onto the ice and went fishing.

On the coast, the diehard surfers don't let the cold stop them. They don't let the rough waves scare them away. In fact, sometimes it "stokes" them even more and they can't get to the surf fast enough. They simply put on their wet suit, they wax their boards and they "hit" it.

They're getting all the way wet no matter how cold or dangerous it appears to be.

By the way... please forgive me for my poor attempt at including some surf talk. As I write this, I'm actually in an airplane in the very middle of the country 30,000 feet in the air and nowhere near real surfers.

Let me try and stick to what I know. Let's continue fishing.

PAPA KAKU

It's not always recommended that you dive into the water to fish. As Christians, we aren't always ready for what's in the water. We should be strong, healthy and spiritually fit for the dangers that lurk beneath the surface of the water.

Many years ago, I was blessed to visit the beautiful island of Oahu, where I was born. While I was there, I spent quite a bit of time with uncles, aunties and cousins.

One gorgeous day, as if there are many days that aren't gorgeous there, I decided to go snorkeling and spear fishing with my cousin. That had all the gear we needed and they spent some time showing me exactly how to use it.

After my safety lesson and some time learning more about the gear, we headed into the water. My heart was pounding and I was super excited. Just seeing the beauty of nature in the ocean was exhilarating. Being able swim with the fish was incredible. So we waded out into the ocean toward the reef we would hunt.

There was no shortage of fish in these waters. I saw little fish around my legs after the very first step into the water. They were just tiny little guys, but aggressive as they swarmed around our legs as if we were going to feed them.

We continued further past the waves until we reached calm in the waters. This was where our coral reef would be. This is where we would dive and find our next meal. The water was much deeper now and things were starting to get real.

I noticed along the way that the deeper we got, the bigger the fish were around us. It was actually a bit frightening. I can't deny, the thought of sharks being able to swim in these same waters crossed my mind several times. The water was over our heads by now and I know for a fact, that sharks can swim into waters as shallow as the wading pools my kids played in as toddlers.

I had to overcome my fears and remind myself, we're fishing. We are in the ocean with an agenda to catch fish. I was armed and I was ready.

As I placed my face mask down into the water, I could see fish every direction I looked. It appeared that this hunt was going to be easy. It's very rare that I get to see how many fish are around before I cast my line. But this time, I wasn't using a fishing line, I was using a spear. This was my first time spear fishing and my adrenaline was pumping.

But, one of the most important lessons my cousins shared with me was that I had to be patient. I have to admit, when staring at that many fish swimming all around me, I thought to myself, "Why wait?" Literally, there were fish brushing right up against me. Then I saw the prize. He came out of nowhere. I was looking forward and a very large and very long fish brushed my side coming from behind me.

I would later realize it was a 'Kaku' or Great Barracuda. I can't remember how long it was, but I remember it was much larger than me. These fish have very large mouths with extremely sharp teeth. But they rarely attack humans. In this case, he swam by me calmly and confidently. His body was so long, it waved through the water as he moved forward ahead of me.

I fought the feeling of, "I'm going to die." and continued swimming the same direction he was swimming. I remember my cousins saying to be patient and not to release the spear too quickly. So I didn't.

I had to swim with the fish for a while before I could release the spear. Swimming with them, calmly and patiently, allowed the fish to get used to my presence around them. The longer I swam with them, the more comfortable they became swimming around me.

Apparently, the fish were quite comfortable at this time because I was surrounded... at least until Papa Kaku swam by. Then the smaller fish darted away in a flash. So I continued following Papa Kaku. I pulled back my spear which was attached to surgical tubing that stretched along the length of my arm. I continued slowly and Papa Kaku continued slowly swimming forward as if I wasn't even there.

In my mind, I thought for sure, I was taking home the prize. My cousins were going to be so proud of me. I had my eye on this giant fish and I was armed and ready. At just the right time, I released my spear and it shot off my arm like a speeding arrow. The spear pierced through the water and headed straight for Papa Kaku. It all happened so quickly, but from what I remember; it shot upward and appeared to pierce the top of the fish right below its dorsal fin.

In a flash, the fish was gone. That was a little confusing, since the spear is attached to surgical tubing which is attached to my wrist. How could the fish disappear if the spear is still attached to my wrist?

The only answer to that question would be, I missed Papa Kaku. But as I swam to retrieve my spear, I noticed it was jerking around erratically and to my surprise, I discovered I missed Papa Kaku, but hit an innocent victim that happened to be swimming on the other side of him. Unfortunately, my prize ended up being a tiny sun fish about the size of my hand.

At least I got something, but I left the water with a much smaller catch than I thought I would. My cousins all had a good laugh and we now have stories to tell for the rest of our lives.

My problem was not that there were no fish. There were plenty of fish to be caught. I can't say I wasn't ready, because I felt more than ready. I trained hard, I had the gear and I was anxious to catch my prize. But, maybe that was my problem all along. I was anxious.

I do feel like our time on this Earth is coming closer and closer to an end, but God's timing is everything! The Bible says, be anxious for nothing, but in all things – PRAY! In that ocean, my heart was racing. I had targets on every fish around me. My spear was ready and I had my eye on the prize. But I was anxious. When you're fishing, you must be patient.

Papa Kaku was starting to get used to me in his waters. It appeared I had earned his trust. But the truth was, he didn't trust me as much as I thought he did and he sensed danger before I could even release it. It was obvious, I didn't wait long enough.

If you're patient enough, eventually the fish will be so comfortable with you that they'll even let you touch them. Once they let you touch them, eventually they'll let you pull them right out of the water with very little to no effort.

When fishing for men, we need to earn their trust. We need to convince them that we aren't out to "get" them. The best thing we can do is love them as God loves them. Then, when the time is right, they'll let you carry them right out of their murky waters and into fresh living waters.

THERE ARE OPEN SEATS AT THE BAR

Today, besides having the privilege of being the lead pastor of one of the greatest churches in America, I also have the honor of helping my buddy with his business. Years ago, he hired me to be his director of business development and that's exactly what I do.

I love the job because it's not a 9 to 5. It allows me to work from home and my schedule is quite flexible. I attend a few trade shows and business conferences each year and mingle with top level executives in hopes of earning their business.

One colleague of mine, I've seen 3 times a year for the last 5 years. He grew up in India as a Muslim but eventually discovered a life with Christ and now enjoys talking about church and ministry with me every time we get together.

One year following our conference, we both had flights home around the same time. So we decided to go to dinner together and I offered to take him to the airport with me after eating.

This particular year I was staying at the Luxor and my buddy agreed to meet me there. We decided to eat at the Mexican restaurant there in the hotel. I was there for almost a week and it had proven to offer amazing food with incredible flavors that you don't get at your local Taco Bell.

Well, we met at the restaurant entrance and approached the desk to request a table. Little did we realize, the restaurant was packed and we had nearly an hour wait time before we would be seated. I guess if it were any other night, an hour wait would not have bothered us at all. But we both had flights to catch and we didn't have an hour to spare.

I shared this fact with the hostess, but to our surprise, that news did not open up any tables. But, she did tell us that the bar was open seating and there were several open seats at the bar.

My friend, knowing I was a pastor, looked at me with a concerned look on his face and hesitantly asked, "Are you OK with sitting in the bar?" I'm sure in his mind he was thinking that I would never be caught dead in a bar. However, we just spent a week conducting business in a city known as "Sin City." A city that boasts, "What happens in Vegas, stays in Vegas." Tell that to the men and women that lost their marriages as a result of indulging in their fleshly desires. Tell that to the one that cannot stop gambling no matter how hard they try and lost everything on the color red or busted with 22.

This was the city we just spent a week in conducting business. And to his surprise, I looked at him and replied, "Yeah man. Let's sit at the bar and eat."

Truth is, I was tired and I had a plane to catch. The last thing I wanted to do was go on a search for another restaurant hoping there was no wait and worst case scenario, stay and wait for a table, but miss my flight. It was time to trust my armor and go all in.

We headed straight to the free seats at the bar and dove right into the menu. As we waited for our food, my friend, as I expected, asked how the church was doing. I love when he asks that question, not because I get to brag on my church, but because I get to brag on my God; the same God he discovered after years of living in a Muslim house.

I began giving him my updates and it appeared he was totally into what I was saying. And as you read this story, it would be natural to think that my friend was a great catch. I would totally understand if you were reading this story and assumed I was fishing for my colleague in an attempt to fully engage him in a life of righteousness and an authentic relationship with Jesus Christ. And if you were thinking that, you would be partially correct. I had my sights on him for a few years and felt like significant progress was being made.

But, even I was surprised to find out there were bigger fish in the sea. I went all in and expected God to fully protect me and open up doors of opportunity to shine a light in the dark bar where there were more non-believers than believers. And opening up doors of opportunity He certainly did.

As I was sharing my church update with my friend, there was man sitting on the other side of him that leaned over the bar past my colleague and shouted at me with a stench of alcohol on his breath. Between the way he smelled and the way he slurred every word, it was quite obvious the man sitting on the other side of my friend was completely drunk.

He leaned over the bar and shouted at me, "If God was here right now, he's strike us all dead and send us to hell." I looked at him, probably with a look of shock on my face and replied, "I sure hope you're wrong man." I went on to share, "I believe God has grace that goes way beyond our understanding." He looked at me and slurred, "No way man, he'd send us all to hell." I continued to share my limited understanding of God's grace and eventually he turned away and we continued to eat our meals.

We finally finished eating and I felt a hand grab my shoulder unexpectedly. I didn't even notice that the drunk man that was sure we were all going to hell finished his meal just before us and was now leaving. On his way out, he grabbed my shoulder with one last word for me.

I turned and looked at him and asked him, "What's up man?" I fully expected him to continue cussing at me or at the very least, remind me that I was going to hell just for stepping foot in this bar. But he surprised me once again.

With the most sober voice, he looked me right in the eyes and said, "I just wanted you to know, I needed to hear everything you had to say." He was referring not just to my comment about grace, but he was listening to my entire church update. He thanked me for everything I was saying and did so with the calmest most sober voice possible. He literally sounded like he was drinking water all night.

As my friend looked on, I looked at the stranger and said, "It's never too late."

I could see him starting to tear up and I knew this was my moment to strike. I was completely submerged and swimming in a sea of sinners. This was the fish I could not let get away. I had to set the hook and I had to do it right then. So I put my hand on his shoulder and asked him if I could pray for him. I reminded him that God cared for him even in the state of mind that he was living in. I shared with him that God knew all of his sin and pre-paid for his forgiveness and redemption.

He agreed to let me pray for him and I led him through a simple prayer of salvation. I say simple because it took a mere 60 seconds to lead him in prayer and send him on his way with a new hope in God that he had never known before.

I set the hook, I reeled him in and I introduced him to a new life with Christ right there, literally at the bar.

That is one fishing trip I will never ever forget.

NOTES

NOTES

- CHAPTER 5 -
ADDITIONAL FISHING TIPS

Additional Fishing Tips

Let me share with you some final fishing tips that just might help you reach more of the lost than ever before.

I've always enjoyed fishing and most of the time I'm pretty confident in my knowledge and skills. But there are always those fishing trips that are simply frustrating. They're not frustrating because I'm not catching fish, but because there are others fishing right next to me catching two to three times more fish than I am. Or often times, I've cast my line a million times without one bite and the guy next to me is catching a fish every other cast.

These are the times that I need to humble myself and take a few tips from the guys catching the fish. By no means am I an expert fisherman of fish or of men, but let me finish this up with a few additional fishing tips for you that has helped me in the past..

CLEAN YOUR GEAR

> *[Luke 5:1-2 NLT] 1 One day as Jesus was preaching on the shore of the Sea of Galilee, great crowds pressed in on him to listen to the word of God. 2 He noticed two empty boats at the water's edge, for the fishermen had left them and were washing their nets.*

I remember fishing and always wondering when I got home how we smelled so awful at the end of the day when we didn't even catch one fish. And after fishing all day, sometimes in direct sunlight, I was often ready to just get home and be with my wife.

But that was easier said than done. You see, not even a simple hug was allowed until I showered and completely rid myself of the awful fish smell that covered every square inch of me.

Of course, it wasn't just me that needed to be cleaned. It was all my gear that needed to be cleaned. In Luke chapter 5, the fishermen at the Sea of Galilee were not in their boats when Jesus was preaching on the shore. Instead, they had left their boats in order to wash their nets.

I find this quite interesting since we also know from this story that these fishermen had not caught any fish. Yet they were found to be washing their equipment.

As a fisher of men, we should be cleaning our gear even when we haven't caught anything in a while. When is the last time you knocked the dust off your Bible? When is the last time we consecrated ourselves and sanctified ourselves as disciples of Christ?

See, as fishermen, we're going to get dirty whether we catch fish or not. It's expected. And when we get home, we clean up. Likewise, as fishers of men, we will often get dirty as well, even when we haven't led anyone to Christ.

How do we get dirty? We don't get dirty in the sense that we swim, smell and act like the fish we're fishing for. Hopefully we've put on the full armor of God before fishing. But as we engage with sinners and enter their environments, we must continually cleanse ourselves and consecrate ourselves before God, presenting ourselves holy and acceptable to the Lord.

> *[Luke 5:3-5 NLT] 3 Stepping into one of the boats, Jesus asked Simon, its owner, to push it out into the water. So he sat in the boat and taught the crowds from there. 4 When he had finished speaking, he said to Simon, "Now go out where it is deeper, and let down your nets to catch some fish." 5 "Master," Simon replied, "we worked hard all last night and didn't catch a thing. But if you say so, I'll let the nets down again."*

Have you ever felt like you've worked day and night with little results? I have many times. Don't be surprised if you work an entire month, year, or lifetime with little results. Sometimes you put your all into something and fail to see the results you were really going for. But no matter what, when God tells you to go out, you go out; even if you've been going out for years with no results.

One of the most frustrating things about fishing with buddies is when you both use the same gear, the same bait, the same everything, yet they catch fish and you don't.

In ministry, you may be doing everything that the big church down the road is doing, but that doesn't mean you'll have the same results. I would gripe and complain all day long when my buddy would be catching fish all day while I caught nothing; even though I was using the exact same gear.

One important tip to remember though; no matter how long you fish with no results, when God tells you to cast your fishing nets, you cast your fishing nets.

Don't ever refuse God because you've come up empty in the past. As fishers of men, we MUST continue fishing, especially when God directs us to cast our nets or our lines.

Jesus was fully aware that these fishermen had been fishing all day with no results. So He gets in the boat with Simon and teaches the crowds from in the boat. Then after He was done teaching, He then tells Simon to let down their nets to catch some fish.

How many of us would have argued with God at this point. I mean, Simon was a professional fisherman. He had been fishing all day and caught nothing. If there was anyone qualified to say there's no fish here, it would have been Simon. In fact, he did tell Jesus that he had fished all day with no results but he didn't let his past results (or lack thereof) determine his obedience.

Again, never ignore the instructions of God based on past disappointments. Remember this; God's instructions ALWAYS lead to positive results.

> *[Luke 5:6 NLT] 6 And this time their nets were so full of fish they began to tear!*

You see when God sends you forth, the game changes. You may have fished one hole for 15 years, but the moment God tells you to lower your nets, you lower your nets one more time. When you obey God and do exactly as He says, you will reap rewards you never expected.

The fishermen who had fished all day and caught nothing had every reason to refuse God and even argue the fact that the fish just were not biting that day.

But that's not what they did. They obeyed God regardless of their recent disappointments and they caught so many fish that their nets began to break. Now that's a serious reward.

MAKE SURE GOD PREPARED YOUR POND

There are a few problems with the way Christians sometimes obey God when it comes to fishing for men.

Many believers who want to be fishers of men are fishing in a fishing hole that God did not prepare for them. Although the water looks good and the elements look perfect, if God did not prepare the fishing hole you are trying to fish in, you may find yourself highly disappointed with your results.

This example may seem silly, but as a fisherman I can testify to a much greater success rate following the proper preparation of my fishing hole.

There were a few regular ponds I used to fish in when I lived in Boise, ID. And without a doubt, the ponds were popular because you often caught your legal limit of fish allowed by the state fish and game. But we weren't always successful.

We would often check the newspaper to see if the fish and game people prepared our fishing pond before we went. They would arrive in a big truck with a giant tank on the back and they would back it right up to the water's edge. The giant tank on the truck was designed to offer a comfortable ride for hundreds of fish if not thousands of fish as they were being transported to what would become their new home. Often, ecologists and other officially really smart people would prepare the water for the fish that were about to be relocated.

But right before they arrived, the fishing results were less than desirable. Sometimes we would fish this pond before they showed up and we would catch nothing. Hours and hours of fishing using every bait in our tackle box and we wouldn't even get a bite. The pond had not been prepared for us and the results truly reflected that fact.

CHANGE BAIT WHEN THEY'RE NOT BITING

There were other times when we wanted to fish so bad we just found any water that was wet. Wait… Is there water that's not wet? Anyway, if there was water, our line was going in. But that was a tough way to fish.

Sometimes as Christians we get excited about doing something for God. Which, that in itself is not bad. However, there often comes a point in time when the desire to do something for God is no longer a desire to do something for God. It can sometimes just be a desire to do something. And if we're not careful, the desire to do something can become motivated by our own selfishness. Now we have a desire to do something for OURSELF.

When that happens, many will stay at a fishing hole using their own techniques way longer than they should be. When I'm out fishing, if I haven't caught something after 5 – 10 casts, I'm moving on; even if I've caught fish there before.

That would be like a pastor who, in the past, may have seen many people come to the Lord through his ministry. Maybe they had a successful season leading many people to the Lord… 25 years ago. But today, there are only a handful of people around that have been saved for 25 years or longer and there isn't really any new fruit coming from the vine any longer.

Sometimes the bait that worked yesterday won't catch a single fish today. You have to look around. You have to ask other fishermen what they're using. You have to change the color of your bait. Change how deep you're fishing. Change the jig.

Don't think for a second that the same bait will work today that worked for you yesterday, last year or even 20 years ago.

Just because you caught fish using certain bait in the past, doesn't mean you'll ever catch a fish again using that same bait.

LEAVE YOUR GEAR FOR GOD'S GEAR

> *11 And when they had brought their ships to land, they forsook all, and followed him.*

These men trusted the Words of Jesus and left their gear to be fishers of men.

God blessed my family with an incredible season of financial blessing. We were blessed to minister to each other through much needed family time. We enjoyed several vacations each year, we bought the cars we loved, we built our first home from the ground up and money was not an issue.

But as much as we enjoyed ministering to each other, we knew it was time to get back in the water and minister to others.

It was time to get fishing again.

One night my wife and I were sitting on our front porch. We loved our home. But something was wrong. I noticed my wife was looking a little saddened. I asked her what was wrong and she replied with tears beginning to form in her eyes. She proceeded to share with me how much she missed our ministry as pastors.

At this point, I began to tear up as I looked past our porch and across our lawn at the beautiful Mercedes Benz I've been enjoying, with all the options and 20" shiny chrome wheels. Now staring at my favorite car, I asked her with conviction in my voice, "Are you willing to give up all of this to follow the call on our lives? Are you willing to give up the cars, the vacations and even this house to fish for men again?"

And without even a hesitation, she replied, "YES!"

So it was decided. We gave up everything we had and basically started over. We laid down our own gear and picked up God's gear!

Sometimes when you decide to go fishing, you need to leave your gear in favor of His.

SET THE TENSION RIGHT

Tension has to be just right once you hook a fish. You can't just reel in as fast and as hard as you can or you risk breaking the line because the tension is too tight. But you can't allow any slack or the fish will spit the hook out.

I remember some fishing trips that were so frustrating. I think the fish were much smarter than I was. Well, I know they were much smarter than I was. I wasn't having a problem catching them; I was just having a problem landing them.

Sometimes we set the tension too tight on a new convert that we just caught. We want to reel them in super fast and the tension is way too tight. We make sure they know they are not to smoke, drink, cuss, party or anything else they "used" to do. And of course, they are expected to be at every church service even if the preacher preaches a 3 hour sermon.

Usually, this kind of fishing will always result in a snapped line. The tension is way too tight for a fish you just caught and they snap your line as quick as they can.

There are other times when we don't want to be offensive, so we give our new convert way too much slack. We forget to lead them into a life of righteousness and we just hope they "get" it. But all too often, there isn't enough tension and they end up spitting the hook out.

Often times you just need to set the tension just right and let the fish run when they feel like running. Don't snap the line back, as you just might break it. You need to keep just the right amount of tension to allow them their space and trust that they will eventually turn back toward you. And when they do, you begin reeling in again keeping that tension just right. Eventually they reach the boat and you net the fish.

MOVE WITH THE FISH

Sometimes you need to move with the fish.

I remember bass fishing around logs and weeds. I often had to move around the bank to avoid getting tangled up around things. In the river, I've literally waded across rapids over waist deep holding my pole above water keeping my fish clear of rocks and logs.

When fishing from a boat, we always had a small trolling motor and when a fish was in, someone would work the trolling motor and move the boat appropriately to keep our line out of trouble.

You don't always see where you're fish is trying to hide under the surface so you need to move with it. You don't know the trials they're facing the temptations they're fighting or the rock they're trying to hide under. Sometimes we ourselves have to put on the full armor of God and go below the surface to know where our fish are hiding. Move with your fish. If you don't, the very rock your fish is hiding behind or the very log they're hunkered down under will snap your line.

BE PREPARED

Sometimes you're not ready to go we're the fish are. You're not properly prepared.

Before my nephew, Bryan Brannon, got married, he decided us guys would go ocean fishing. I was excited. I bought a hat from the charter company and everything. As we launched the boat, we started preparing our lines and claiming our spot on the boat. Well, everyone but me. You see, I wasn't prepared for ocean fishing. I am a total light weight when it comes to motion sickness. About 15 minutes out to sea, I was already feeling the effects of the rolling waves. To make a long story short, I never touched my pole. I was puking my guts out over the side of the boat the entire trip. While my friends were pulling in fish, I was feeding them over the side.

And when I had nothing else to throw up, I just went through the motions of throwing up. That was even worst. Towards the end of the fishing time, I eventually curled up in a ball in the middle of the boat and closed my eyes.

I just wanted this fishing adventure to end. But I was so sick, the adventure stuck with me for nearly four days. I couldn't ride an elevator, I couldn't swing on a swing and even riding shotgun in the car was a challenge for me. This was the result of not being prepared.

If you're going to fish for men, make sure you go fishing totally prepared to fish where they are. If you don't prepare yourself for the worst, you may get sick before you even see the fish.

YOU DON'T ALWAYS CATCH WHAT YOU'RE FISHING FOR

Once when I was a kid, I went fishing on the ocean with a friend of mine and we were fishing for sun fish. All of a sudden my pole nearly snapped and I thought I had hooked a whopper of a sun fish until I got it to the boat and discovered I had caught a black tip shark.

When you're out there fishing for men, you might have your eyes set on one person and God totally gives you another. How often are we fishing for specific types of people and we land another?

Fishing for people is not like fishing for fish in this respect. We DON'T throw any back! Be prepared to catch fish you weren't fishing for. When you're a fisher of men, every fish you catch for Jesus is a keeper; no matter what they look like, smell like or act like.

KNOW YOUR FISH

My wife and I were the pastors of a little church in Des Moines, Iowa for a time. One of my favorite parts of being in Iowa was the incredible fishing. It seemed like wherever there was water, there was good fishing.

One afternoon, we were visiting a church family for lunch and they had a large pond on their property. We decided to throw our lines in and catch a few bass. They were hitting hard and we had a blast catching them.

I landed one bass that looked to be the perfect largemouth bass. It was large, it was heavy and it was beautiful. We took that fish home and we were ready for the greatest fish fry ever.

We began to clean this fish and as we cut through the fish to prepare it, we noticed little white things in the translucent meat. Then as we observed a little closer, we noticed these little white things were actually moving.

Turns out that every fish we caught had some kind of worm living inside of its flesh. Needless to say, we didn't eat that fish. From the outside, we were proud of these fish. But once we took a look at the inside, we nearly threw up in our mouths.

Some of us are really proud of the fish we've caught. We're filling our churches with fish that look amazing on the outside. However, we need to ask God to reveal to us what's on the inside of the fish we're landing. Not to condemn them should we find moving white worms inside, but in order to know what we've landed before we cut them open and try to elevate them too quickly.

NOTES

- CHAPTER 6 -
GET YOUR GEAR!

Get Your Gear!

> *[Mat 4:19 NKJV] 19 Then He said to them, "Follow Me, and I will make you fishers of men."*

Some of us don't go fishing because we don't feel qualified. We struggle with feeling inadequate. We sometimes feel like we're not good enough, we're not smart enough, we're not pretty enough or we're not spiritual enough.

Many believe the fishermen are the pastors, the leaders, the teachers, the Bishop.

The pastor isn't a fisherman because he's a pastor, but because he follows Jesus and Jesus MAKES him.

The leader isn't a fisherman because he's a leader, but because he follows Jesus and Jesus MAKES him.

The teacher isn't a fisherman because he's a teacher, but because he follows Jesus and Jesus MAKES him.

The bishop isn't a fisherman because he's a bishop, but because he follows Jesus and Jesus MAKES him.

Spurgeon preached it this way...

WHEN CHRIST CALLS US by his grace we ought not only to remember what we are, but we ought also to think of what he can make us. It is, "Follow me, and I will make you." We should repent of what we have been, but rejoice in what we may be. It is not "Follow me, because of what you are already." It is not "Follow me, because you may make something of yourselves;" but, "Follow me, because of what I will make you."

God wants us to follow so He can make us! This is really special because we don't need to be pre-qualified, we don't need certificates on the wall or degrees on our shelf. We just need to follow. We can't make ourselves and nobody else can make us either. We need to follow HIM and He will "make" us.

God isn't calling us to be fishers of men because of who we are, but because of who He can make us.

One year on a family vacation, we decided to take the kids fishing. We went to the local store and let the kids pick out their gear. Of course, my son Kameron always had to be different, so he chose a 10' cane pole. It didn't even have a real. You just tied your line to it and held it way over the water, hopefully where the fish were.

My son was no professional fisherman. He didn't even take the most common equipment. For the record, he did NOT look like a fisherman. But, with that crazy 10' pole, he caught more fish than all the rest of the family put together and caught the largest fish he had ever caught in his life.

God didn't call Peter and his boys to join Him in ministry because they were eloquent speakers, had multiple degrees or were the most influential. He called them to FOLLOW because He knew what He could MAKE them!

God isn't calling us because of who we are, but because of who He can make us become.

> [Psa 100:3 NKJV] 3 Know that the LORD, He [is] God; [It is] He [who] has made us, and not we ourselves; [We are] His people and the sheep of His pasture.

[Psa 139:14 NKJV] 14 I will praise You, for I am fearfully [and] wonderfully made; Marvelous are Your works, And [that] my soul knows very well.

[Eph 2:10 NKJV] 10 For we are His workmanship, created in Christ Jesus for good works, which God prepared beforehand that we should walk in them.

God has fearfully and wonderfully made you. And God is fearfully and wonderfully making you.

NOTES

FINAL THOUGHTS

God already knows the type of fishing we are to do. He has already prepared the fish beforehand. He is making us to be the fishers of men He needs us to be.

> *[Eph 4:23-24 NKJV] 23 and be renewed in the spirit of your mind, 24 and that you put on the new man which was created according to God, in true righteousness and holiness.*

With a renewed mind, we can cast our nets into the deep and fill our boats overflowing.

> *[Hbr 10:35 NKJV] 35 Therefore do not cast away your confidence, which has great reward.*

Will you FOLLOW and let Him MAKE you? Let God make you a fisher of men.

Don't ignore the fish because of who you think you are or are not! Don't get stuck without your gear feeling inadequate. Go get your gear and **LET'S GO FISHING!**

NOTES

NOTES

Made in the USA
Charleston, SC
18 October 2016